W   RY

P. O. BOX 40
14177 MARKET STREET
WALNUT GROVE, CA 95690

SEP   2003

10/03- Ø
1/05- Ø

Davy Crockett

History Maker Bios

Elaine Marie Alphin

LERNER PUBLICATIONS COMPANY • MINNEAPOLIS

*For Art, who's forever looking ahead to the next frontier
on his horizon*

Illustrations by Tim Parlin

Text copyright © 2003 by Elaine Marie Alphin
Illustrations copyright © 2003 by Lerner Publications Company

All rights reserved. International copyright secured. No part of this book may be
reproduced, stored in a retrieval system, or transmitted in any form or by any
means—electronic, mechanical, photocopying, recording, or otherwise—without
the prior written permission of Lerner Publications Company, except for the
inclusion of brief quotations in an acknowledged review.

Lerner Publications Company
A division of Lerner Publishing Group
241 First Avenue North
Minneapolis, MN 55401 U.S.A.

Website address: www.lernerbooks.com

Library of Congress Cataloging-in-Publication Data

Alphin, Elaine Marie.
    Davy Crockett / by Elaine Marie Alphin.
      p.   cm. — (History maker bios)
    Includes bibliographical references and index.
    Summary: Describes the life and accomplishments of David Crockett, the
famous frontier settler, congressman, and defender of the Alamo.
    ISBN: 0–8225–0393–X (lib. bdg. : alk. paper)
    1. Crockett, Davy, 1786–1836—Juvenile literature. 2. Pioneers—Tennessee—
Biography—Juvenile literature. 3. Frontier and pioneer life—Tennessee—
Juvenile literature. 4. Tennessee—Biography—Juvenile literature. 5.
Legislators—United States—Biography—Juvenile literature. 6. United States—
Congress—House—Biography—Juvenile literature. 7. Alamo (San Antonio,
Tex.)—Siege, 1836—Juvenile literature. [1. Crockett, Davy, 1786–1836.
2. Pioneers. 3. Legislators.] I. Title. II. Series.
    F436.C95 A75 2003
    976.8'04'092—dc21   2002000450

Manufactured in the United States of America
1 2 3 4 5 6 – JR – 08 07 06 05 04 03

TABLE OF CONTENTS

INTRODUCTION

David Crockett spent most of his life exploring and hunting across America's untamed frontier. The stories he told of his adventures sounded like tall tales come to life. He claimed that he could whip his weight in wildcats or hug a bear too close for comfort—and live to tell about it.

The real David couldn't do all that. But he still lived an exciting life. He cleared wilderness to start farms. He scouted for Tennessee soldiers in a war against Indians. He served in Congress, where he worked to help poor people. He wrote books. And he died fighting to free Texas from Mexico in 1836. Along the way, he became an American legend.

This is his story.

1 WILD BOY

In 1794, when David Crockett was eight, he told his father he wanted to hunt for supper. The Crockett family ate what they grew on their land or hunted in the Tennessee woods. David wanted to hunt like his older brothers.

John Crockett said he couldn't afford to waste rifle balls on a boy's missed shots. A flood had just swept away Crockett's mill, and he owed money.

David promised he would make every shot count. So his father let him use a long Kentucky rifle. It was almost as long as David was tall! But each day, David got only one ball and enough powder to shoot it. If he hit something, he'd have supper. If he missed, he'd go hungry.

David aimed carefully with that one ball. Sometimes he missed, but most days he brought home supper. And he learned to love roaming the woods.

Long rifles were built to be more accurate than other hunting guns. A hunter could be more sure of hitting a target with a long rifle.

David drove Jacob Siler's cattle four hundred miles. He was paid about six dollars for his work.

Then John Crockett moved the family to wilder country in western Tennessee. He opened an inn for hunters and travelers. But he still owed people money. As soon as his sons were old enough to work, he hired them out.

When David was twelve, his father hired him out to Jacob Siler. David's job was to help drive a herd of cattle to Virginia. When he got there, Siler said that David had to keep working for him. David stayed. But he missed his parents terribly.

One day, David saw some men he remembered from Tennessee. He told them he was homesick. They said his father hadn't bound him to Siler forever. If he could leave that night, he could go home with them.

David lay in bed, waiting for his chance. Finally he crept outside, only to see heavy snow falling. "The whole sky was hid by the falling snow. . . , " he recalled. "I had to guess at my way to the big road, which was about a half mile from the house."

DAVID OR DAVY?

Most people today know David Crockett as Davy Crockett. But in his lifetime, David wasn't called Davy. The nickname sprang up soon after his death. In the 1950s, a popular television show dressed "Davy" in a coonskin cap. The real David wore a broad-brimmed felt hat.

If David didn't reach the men in time, he would have to stay in Virginia. But he had learned the countryside pretty well. In spite of the snow, he managed to find the road and follow it to the meeting place.

After David got home, his parents sent him to a one-room school. But school wasn't much better than working for Jacob Siler. David fought with another boy. He started hiding in the woods every day.

When John Crockett found out, he threatened to whip David and send him back to school. Instead, David ran away. He was still only twelve years old.

Parents had to pay to send their children to a frontier school. Many children never went to school at all.

John Crockett's inn, rebuilt in modern times

For three years, David worked on his own in Virginia, Maryland, and Tennessee. He drove cattle, worked as a farmhand, and almost signed on as a ship's cabin boy. He loved being on his own, but he missed the frontier.

David came home to the Crockett inn when he was fifteen. He didn't tell anyone who he was. He just went inside like a guest. He sat in the shadows, watching his family, until everyone sat down to dinner. Then his older sister Betsy recognized the stranger. She jumped up and hugged him, crying, "Here is my lost brother."

John Crockett still owed money, so he hired David out again. David obeyed his father and did the work. But the next time, he chose his own job. He hired himself out to John Kennedy, a farmer. Then he learned that his father owed Kennedy money, too! David had to work for six months to pay that debt.

David's father cried when he learned that David had paid his debt with six months of hard farmwork.

David was ready to strike out on his own. He wanted a home and a wife to share it with him. He fell in love with John Kennedy's niece. But she was already getting married. David thought she might have chosen him if he had been educated. He wished he'd stayed in school.

Maybe it wasn't too late to get some education. One of Kennedy's sons taught school, and David struck a deal with him. David worked two days a week and went to school four days. In six months, he learned to read and write pretty well.

David tried again. He decided to marry Margaret Elder, a girl his family knew. She agreed, then changed her mind and married someone else. All of his hard work and hopes had come to nothing again. Heartbroken at age nineteen, David decided he "was only born for hardships, misery, and disappointment."

2 HUNTER AND SCOUT

David did not stay disappointed. One afternoon in 1806, he got lost in the woods. He ran into Polly Finley, a girl he had met at a dance. She was lost, too.

David and Polly took shelter in an empty cabin, and David spent the night talking her into marrying him. They were married the next month on August 16, one day before David's twentieth birthday.

The Crocketts had two sons, John and William. Then, in 1811, David decided that their part of Tennessee was too crowded. He moved his family farther west and cleared land for a farm on the frontier. There a daughter, Margaret, was born in 1812.

Like many frontier women, Polly had a spinning wheel and loom for making fabric.

David on a bear-
hunting trip

David had everything most men would want. But he was restless. He was more interested in hunting than farming. Most days he went out with his dogs. He brought home wild turkeys and deer for the supper table, and bears for warm winter rugs.

On his hunting trips, David met some of the few Cherokee, Creek, and Choctaw Indians who still lived in the area. Most had been pushed west as settlers like the Crocketts arrived. David got on fine with the Indians he met. That changed in 1813.

That summer, white soldiers attacked and killed some Creek Indians in Alabama. Creek warriors struck back at Fort Mims. They burned the fort and killed nearly five hundred soldiers and settlers. They even killed women and children who had gathered inside the fort for safety.

When David heard this news, he wanted to fight. In September, he joined the Tennessee Volunteer Mounted Riflemen. He worked three months as a scout, searching for enemies. He also hunted for the soldiers' meals.

The Creek Indians included several different tribes. They lived by farming, fishing, and hunting.

David took part in a few small fights but no large battles. He did see one terrible sight—a whole town of Creek Indians killed in revenge for the attack on Fort Mims. The Creeks surrendered to General Andrew Jackson in March 1814. By then David was back home. He earned sixty-five dollars for his service.

A VOLUNTEER ARMY

General Andrew Jackson's army was made up of volunteers from Alabama and Tennessee. In the 1800s, many people thought that a national army would give the American government too much power over the states. Having volunteer armies in each state let local settlers make their own decisions. But it also meant they had to fight to protect their families and farms instead of depending on the government for help.

Corn was an important food for both Indians and white settlers.

Family and farming seemed dull after hunting and fighting. David stayed home only long enough to plant and harvest his crops. In September, he went off to fight unfriendly Creeks in Florida.

David found he would rather trade with the Creeks than kill them. He offered one Creek man a silver dollar for a hat full of corn. The man said he'd swap corn for rifle balls instead. He seemed friendly enough. David decided that the Creek probably wouldn't shoot him, so he swapped.

Finally David headed home. When he reached the farm, he found Polly dying from swamp fever. She probably had a disease called malaria.

After Polly died, David missed her terribly. To make things worse, he couldn't handle the farm and his small children. He needed a new wife.

A widow named Elizabeth Patton lived nearby with her young son and daughter. David thought that perhaps he and Elizabeth could help each other out. She agreed. They married in 1815.

Elizabeth had a good-sized farm, but the land had bad swamps. David decided to sell it and buy better land, farther west. But where?

3 PIONEER IN POLITICS

David believed in thinking a problem through, then acting. He liked to tell people, "Be always sure you're right— then go ahead!" Now he thought about Alabama, where he had spent some of his scouting days. Maybe it would be the right place for his family.

Exploring the wilderness could be dangerous, but David loved the adventure.

To find out, David went exploring with three other settlers. He left Elizabeth in Tennessee with her two children, his three children, and a new baby on the way.

David and his friends had bad luck. One was bitten by a poisonous snake. Then the horses ran off. David went after the horses, but he couldn't catch them. Tired and alone, he had an attack of malaria. He survived and went straight home. Alabama was *not* the right place for him!

Instead, David moved his family to Shoal Creek, Tennessee, in 1816. He built a mill and a gunpowder factory. Shoal Creek was a rough place. At first, the town had no government at all. When people disagreed about property or accused each other of crimes, they had to wait for a traveling judge to come and hear their cases.

In 1818, David decided to help his neighbors by becoming a justice of the peace. His job would be to settle arguments so that people wouldn't have to wait for the traveling judge.

David's mill worked much like this pioneer mill did. Water turned a large wheel, which ground corn.

David built this bench for the Tennessee courthouse where he served as a justice of the peace.

His trickiest case involved some hogs. One man said that another had stolen his hogs. He could prove that the hogs were his—they were marked with his brand. David made the thief pay for the hogs. But the owner had never registered his brand as the law said farmers must do. So the men had to split the court costs. Both agreed this was fair.

David bragged that no one ever tried to have his judgments reversed. As he explained, he simply depended on his own "natural born sense, and not on law learning" to decide what was right.

People liked David's "natural born sense," and he noticed. In 1821, he decided to run for a position in Tennessee's legislature, or lawmaking assembly.

Running for office turned out to be fun. David traveled around the county, speaking to voters. He sized up each audience and gave them what they wanted. If they were tired of listening to speeches, he told a joke or a funny story about his adventures. If they were thirsty, he bought drinks.

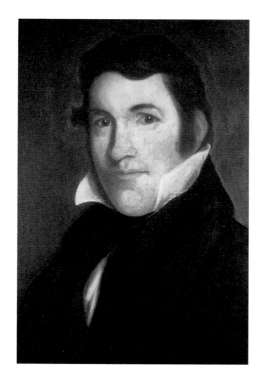

David in the 1820s, dressed up for government work

David knew that his wealthy, well-educated opponent "didn't think, for a moment, that he was in any danger from an ignorant back-woods bear hunter." But the bear hunter's friendly campaigning did the trick. David won the election!

Even though he had joked his way to victory, when David got to the legislature he worked seriously for what he believed. Most of all, he was concerned about the hardworking people who had settled the Tennessee frontier.

Campaign Jokes

In 1823, David ran for the legislature against a doctor named William Butler. He used humor to point out how different Butler was from most frontier folks. David joked that Butler walked on rugs made of better material than the dresses frontier women wore! Once again, his good humor won the hearts and votes of Tennessee settlers, and he won the election.

When frontier settlers claimed a piece of wilderness, they would clear it for farming. Later, government officials would come to map the land. They often gave that land to new owners—even though settlers already lived there. David tried to pass laws to help settlers stay on land they had cleared.

While David worried about lawmaking, he had his own problems. A flood destroyed his factory and mill. David cleared land for a a new home along the Obion River in northwestern Tennessee. In 1822, he moved Elizabeth and their nine children there.

The flood left David owing money to people, just like his father had years ago. But David didn't hire out his sons to pay his debts. Instead, Elizabeth took over the family business. She settled their debts, leaving David free for a new adventure.

4 HUNTING FOR VOTES

People were talking about David Crockett. He had done a good job in the Tennessee legislature. Maybe he should represent the whole state in the United States Congress.

David agreed. He liked protecting the rights of everyday farmers—and being popular and important at the same time. He lost his first run for Congress in 1824, but he tried again in the next election.

David traveled from town to town, meeting people and listening to their problems. He didn't promise to fix everything voters complained about. In fact, he talked more about his hunting and war adventures than his work making laws.

David's stories and jokes made politics entertaining for frontier voters.

David once claimed to have killed 105 bears in a single winter.

Some of David's amazing tales weren't quite true. To impress his listeners, he added a few months and a few battles to his time in the military. He told some fantastic hunting stories, too.

Once, he claimed, he had a fine day with his double-barreled shotgun. He shot a whole flock of geese with one barrel and a deer with the other. The shotgun kicked so hard that it knocked David back into a river. He climbed out with his pockets full of fish. Their weight popped off his coat buttons. One button killed a bear, and the other killed a squirrel. David filled his game bag without ever reloading—or so he said.

Voters knew that David was just telling tall tales, but they believed he would be a good congressman. They had already seen how he spoke up for them in the legislature. Besides, people liked him.

David won the 1827 election. At age forty-one, he headed to Washington, D.C. He found Washington very different from Tennessee. David's down-home charm made him awkward in the capital's elegant social scene.

MEET DAVID CROCKETT

One tall tale tells how David greeted a crowd on his way to Congress. He bragged, "I'm that same David Crockett, fresh from the backwoods, half-horse, half-alligator, a little touched with the snapping-turtle; can wade the Mississippi, leap the Ohio, ride upon a streak of lightning, and slip without a scratch down a honey locust [tree]."

David's confusion with a waiter made him the target of jokes in Washington, D.C.

At a fancy party, people laughed when David got mad at a waiter who cleared his plate. David thought the waiter was stealing his food. When finger bowls were set out for washing, he drank the water. He tried to ignore the laughter, but it was hard.

David wanted people in the government to learn about the issues that mattered to poor Tennessee settlers. He expected help from Andrew Jackson, his old general from the Creek War. Jackson was elected president in 1828. He claimed he wanted to help ordinary people like David's friends back in Tennessee.

Like David, President Andrew Jackson grew up in a frontier log cabin. He was the first president to come from such a humble background.

David tried to pass laws to protect settlers' land rights and improve ship traffic on Tennessee rivers. He also wanted to let the Creek, Choctaw, and Cherokee Indians keep their land in western Tennessee. But supporting David's ideas would have made trouble for President Jackson with other politicians. So he refused to help.

Even worse, Jackson still expected David to support his own ideas. David refused. As he explained, "I bark at no man's bid. I will never come and go, and fetch and carry, at the whistle of the great man in the White House no matter who he is."

David decided to let the world know who he was and what he stood for. Another congressman, Thomas Chilton of Kentucky, helped him write a book about his life on the Tennessee frontier. The book became very popular, and in 1834 David toured several northern cities to talk about it. He enjoyed the fuss that his many fans made over him.

Things weren't so easy in Washington. David didn't understand the way one congressman would promise to vote for someone else's idea if that man would vote for his. David wouldn't trade votes, so he made enemies.

Back home, Tennessee voters decided that a congressman who couldn't get things done was no use to them. In 1835, they sent a different man to Congress.

5 REMEMBER THE ALAMO

Hurt and angry at losing the election, David wanted to leave Tennessee and go to a new frontier—Texas. Elizabeth didn't want to move, but David thought she'd change her mind if he found a good place to live.

In 1835, Texas wasn't part of the United States. It was claimed by Mexico, but many of its settlers believed it should be an independent country. This wild, free land sounded like the perfect place for David Crockett.

He set off in November. When he got to Texas, he liked what he saw. The country around the Red River had good water, huge forests, and rich land.

The rich land along the Red River attracted many American settlers like David.

General Antonio Lopéz de Santa Anna wanted Texas to remain part of Mexico.

David went to buy land from a Texas official named Sam Houston. But Houston wasn't in his land office. He was busy raising volunteers to face a Mexican army. Mexico's president, General Antonio Lopéz de Santa Anna, planned to fight to keep Texas part of Mexico.

Many Texas settlers asked for David's help in this new fight. They had read his book about his life and admired his bravery. Now they gave parties in his honor and begged him to join their cause.

The Alamo was built for Spanish missionaries, people who tried to spread the Catholic religion to Indians.

David agreed that the Texas settlers should be free. Here was a chance for him to live up to his own image. He would be a brave soldier and hunter who could defeat any odds.

David got a group of Tennessee volunteers to follow him to San Antonio, Texas. They marched to the Alamo. This walled fort had once been a mission, a place where the Catholic religion was taught to Indians. Now it was filled with Texas defenders.

David and his volunteers reached the Alamo on February 8, 1836. They joined the fort's commanders, William Travis and Jim Bowie, and their men. The defenders threw a party to celebrate the famous bear hunter's arrival.

Travis and Bowie believed that if the Mexicans took the Alamo, Texas would fall. They were determined to face the approaching army, whatever the cost.

The Alamo as it looks today, in modern San Antonio

As the Mexicans marched closer, Travis sent messengers begging for more men. Then Santa Anna surrounded the Alamo. He raised a blood-red flag. The Mexicans would take no prisoners.

David wasn't worried. He had lost an election or two, but he had never lost a fight. He cheerfully told the Texans tall tales about his triumphs. His enthusiasm raised their spirits. But everyone knew that unless more help arrived, the coming battle would be to the death.

A LINE IN THE SAND

Legend has it that David and the other Alamo defenders had a chance to leave the fort. On March 5, William Travis told his men to get ready to fight for their lives. Then he drew a line in the sand. Everyone who would stay and fight should cross the line, he said. Anyone else could try to escape. Only one man, Louis Rose, refused to cross the line. He escaped and lived to tell the tale.

The battle for the Alamo was fierce and deadly.

Santa Anna bombarded the Alamo with cannons for two weeks. A small force arrived to help the defenders, increasing their number to about 189. But 1,800 Mexican soldiers attacked at dawn on March 6, 1836.

Twice, defenders under Travis forced the Mexicans back from the Alamo's north wall. David and his men turned attackers back on the south side. But Mexican soldiers swept over the eastern wall.

David and the other defenders followed their plan. They fell back into the fort's long barracks and made a last stand. Santa Anna showed no mercy. Every Alamo defender, including David, died that day. When the fighting was over, Santa Anna ordered the bodies of the defenders to be burned.

The heroes of the Alamo did not die in vain. A few weeks later, Texas won its freedom. It became a separate country, the Republic of Texas. Several years later, in 1845, Texas joined the United States as the twenty-eighth state.

The Texas state flag also served as the national flag for the Republic of Texas from 1839 to 1845.

David Crockett was more than a tall tale of his own invention. He was a man of action. He decided what was right, and then he did it—whether it was getting an education in order to get a wife, or getting votes in order to help Tennessee farmers.

David knew that war was coming in Texas. He could have gone back home to Tennessee and safety. But he chose to stay and fight for what he believed.

David Crockett spent years of his life making up tall tales about himself as an American hero. In the end, he lived up to the legend he had created.

TIMELINE

DAVID CROCKETT
WAS BORN ON
AUGUST 17, 1786.

In the year . . .

1798	David's father hired him out to drive cattle from Tennessee to Virginia.	Age 12
1799	he ran away from home for three years.	
1806	he married Polly Finley.	
1813	he served under Andrew Jackson in a war against Creek Indians.	Age 27
1815	Polly died.	
	he married Elizabeth Patton.	
1818	he began to hear cases as a justice of the peace.	
1821	he was elected to the Tennessee legislature.	Age 35
	a flood destroyed his factory and mill.	
1822	he moved his family to northwestern Tennessee.	
1824	he ran for Congress and lost.	
1827	he was elected to Congress.	Age 41
1828	Andrew Jackson was elected president.	
1834	he published a book about his life.	
	he toured northern cities to sell his book.	
1835	he lost his seat in Congress.	
	he set off to find a new home in Texas.	
1836	he decided to join the fight for Texas independence.	Age 49
	he brought a group of Tennessee soldiers to the Alamo.	
	he died fighting Mexican soldiers in the Alamo on March 6.	

How Did David Crockett Die?

One story of David's death tells how he was surrounded by Mexican soldiers in the Alamo barracks. David fought to the last, swinging his rifle like a club when there was no time to reload and shoot. But there is another story.

A Mexican officer claimed that David was captured with five other soldiers. David tried to talk his way out, just as he had talked his way into Congress. But the Mexicans were ordered to kill the prisoners. Just before his death, David is said to have attacked General Santa Anna with his bare hands. Even today, no one knows for sure how David Crockett died—except that he died to help make Texas settlers free. Today he is an official "Texas Treasure."

An artist's vision of the death of David Crockett

FURTHER READING

NONFICTION
Burgan, Michael. *The Alamo.* Mankato, MN: Compass Point, 2001. Maps, photographs, and paintings depict the battle that led to David Crockett's death.

Newman, Shirlee P. *The Creek.* Danbury, CT: Franklin Watts, 1996. Describes the history and modern life of the Creek Indians, including the Creek War of 1813–1814.

FICTION
Garland, Sherry. *Voices of the Alamo.* New York: Scholastic, 2001. The story of the Alamo is told through the imagined voices of David and others who lived it.

Kellogg, Steven. *Sally Ann Thunder Ann Whirlwind Crockett.* New York: William Morrow & Company, 1995. A bear-wrestling, fast-talking frontier girl captures David's heart in a story inspired by folk tales of the 1800s.

Schanzer, Rosalyn. *Davy Crockett Saves the World.* New York: HarperCollins, 2001. In this tall tale, Crockett saves America from a collision with a comet from space.

WEBSITES

The Alamo
<www.thealamo.org> This website presents the history of the Alamo and its defenders, including David Crockett, as well as a photo tour of the modern Alamo grounds.

Davy Crockett Birthplace State Historic Area
<http://www.state.tn.us/environment/parks/davyshp/> The log cabin where Crockett grew up has been restored and preserved as a state park, which includes a museum.

SELECT BIBLIOGRAPHY

Burke, James Wakefield. *David Crockett: The Man Behind the Myth.* Austin, TX: Eakin Press, 1984.

Crockett, David. *A Narrative of the Life of David Crockett of Tennessee.* 1834. Reprint, edited by James A. Shackford and Stanley J. Folmsbee. Knoxville, TN: University of Tennessee Press, 1973.

Derr, Mark. *The Frontiersman: The Real Life and the Many Legends of Davy Crockett.* New York: William Morrow & Company, 1993.

Groneman, Bill. *Death of a Legend: The Myth and Mystery Surrounding the Death of Davy Crockett.* Plano, TX: Republic of Texas Press, 1999.

Kilgore, Daniel Edmond. *How Did Davy Die?* College Station, TX: Texas A&M University Press, 1978.

Lofaro, Michael. *Crockett at Two Hundred: New Perspectives on the Man and the Myth.* Knoxville, TN: University of Tennessee Press, 1989.

Lofaro, Michael, ed. *Davy Crockett: The Man, the Legend, the Legacy, 1786–1986.* Knoxville, TN: University of Tennessee Press, 1985.

Long, Jeff. *Duel of Eagles: The Mexican and U.S. Fight for the Alamo.* New York: William Morrow & Company, 1990.

Shackford, James A. *David Crockett: The Man and the Legend.* Chapel Hill, NC: University of North Carolina Press, 1956.

INDEX

Acknowledgments

For photographs and artwork: © Burstein Collection/CORBIS, p. 4; © Art Alphin/Renee Weddle/Independent Picture Service, p. 7; © North Wind Picture Archives, pp. 8, 10, 16, 17, 22, 32, 33, 41; © Sally Baker Bennett/Crockett Tavern Museum, p. 11; © Giraudon/Art Resource, NY, p. 12; © Edward Owen/Art Resource, NY, p. 15; © Jim Simondet/Independent Picture Service, p. 19; © N. Carter/North Wind Picture Archives, p. 23; © Tennessee State Museum, Tennessee Historical Society Collection, p. 24; © Tennessee State Museum Collection, p. 25; © Bettmann/CORBIS, pp. 29, 37, 43; Texas State Library and Archives Commission, p. 30; © A. J. Copley/Visuals Unlimited, p. 36; © A. A. M. Van der Heyden Collection/Independent Picture Service, p. 39; © CORBIS, p. 38; © Richard Cummins/CORBIS, p. 42; © Univeristy of Tennessee Library/Special Collections, p. 45. Front cover, © Bettmann/CORBIS. Back cover, © Renee Weddle/Independent Picture Service.

For quoted material: pp. 9, 11, 13, 21, 24, 26, *Crockett, David. A Narrative of the Life of David Crockett of Tennessee.* Reprint, edited by James A. Shackford and Stanley J. Folmsbee. Knoxville, TN: University of Tennessee Press, 1973; p. 31, Derr, Mark. *The Frontiersman.* New York: William Morrow & Company, 1993; p. 33, Crockett, David. *An Account of Colonel Crockett's Tour to the North and Down East.* Philadelphia: Carey, Hart, and Company, 1835.